The Four Seasons of

Hide and Seek

Written by Christi and Jason Salyer

Illustrated by Caitlyn Kingsbury

Copyright © 2020 Text by Christi and Jason Salyer

Copyright © 2020 Illustrations by Caitlyn Kingsbury

All rights reserved. No part of this publication may be reproduced, distributed, or transmitted in any form or by any means, including photocopying, recording, or other electronic or mechanical methods, without the prior written permission of the publisher, except in the case of brief quotations embodied in critical reviews and certain other noncommercial uses permitted by copyright law. For permission requests, write to the publisher, addressed "Attention: Permissions Coordinator," at the email address below.

salyerchristi@gmail.com

ISBN: 978-0-578-63716-7

First printing edition 2020.

Dear turkey birds,

It is challenging to put into words how grateful we are for the memories being created as we watch and help the three of you grow up. Having three best friends to adventure with, wrestle with, and read bedtime stories to have been the joy of our lives. Despite our best efforts to keep you from growing up, we know that it is hopeless. One day you will be all grown up and not need us to remove the ouchie pokeys or get the glass off of the top shelf. One day you will have little turkeys of your own. We hope that you have fond memories of us when you read this book to them.

To our family and friends who have championed our endeavors, the hardest being parenthood, with a sculpture of memories etched in laughter, oddity, hardships and experience.

Love, Christi and Jason, aka Mom and Dad

To my wonderfully supportive family and friends for the encouragement, wisdom, and endless laughter.

To Michael, the love of my life, thank you for your love, support, and guidance as you have walked with me on this journey.

-Caitlyn Kingsbury

Hide and Seek Instructional

Let's explore the alphabet in a different way.
First, sing the song and then we can play.

Go to the first page and you will see,
The alphabet is hidden so that you can seek.

It is important to say each big and little letter out loud,
so you can learn it and make yourself proud!

Make sure to say each letter in a fun and exciting way.
It might help you remember it if you do it every day.

Winter, spring, summer, and fall are called seasons in which you will learn about.
Learning is so fun, it will make you want to shout!

Learning surrounds us in so many fun ways.
It's easy to create simple games so that your child can play.

Have fun and enjoy this book.
Please place a review and share with your family and friends.
Let them have a look.

The winter **air** is cold and dry.
It is the perfect condition for snow to fly.

The **bugs** stop their **buzzing**
and **bears** start hibernation.
Animals, like geese and elk, have already begun
their winter migration.

The **clever** arctic fox changes its fur from brown to white.
It blends in with the snow to stay out of sight.

The branches are empty on **deciduous** trees. When the air becomes cold they lose all of their leaves.

Evergreen trees, like a spruce and a pine, do not lose their leaves during the wintertime.

When the winter air drops below 32 degrees, the ponds and lakes start to **freeze**.

The **gardens** will grow and birds start to sing,
All will celebrate the arrival of spring.

Hibernating bears have a rumble in their tummy. They awake in the spring to find something yummy. **Insects** like the honeybee, collect nectar and pollen to make honey for its colony.

The **jumping** frogs leap out of hibernation.
They sing a loud song to begin their mating celebration.

Kale and spinach will grow next to beans.
Soon they will be ready for a salad of greens.

The **life** of a butterfly begins as an egg.
It creates a cocoon and then pops out its head.

When **mallards molt** they lose the gift of flight. Soon their feathers grow back shiny and bright.

The **nests** of blue gills are made to protect eggs. They are dug with their fins because they do not have legs.

The **ocean** receives heat from the sun. The combination of wind and sunlight can make the beach warm and fun.

The process of **photosynthesis** (pho-to-syn-the-sis) starts with the suns light.
It is absorbed by a plant's chlorophyll (clor-o-fill) during the day and grows faster at night.

Quiet summers are seldom because the season is full of sound. Insects are singing and thunder storms abound.

After a warm summer rain the **robin** hops and searches.
He hunts for worms that have reached the ground's surface.

Snakes are most active between eighty and ninety degrees. They eat many pests that can carry disease.

The maple **trees** begin to conserve their energy. They slow their production of chlorophyll, giving a burst of color to the autumn leaves.

Under the fall trees are blankets of leaves.
They are dropped to the ground to conserve energy.

The bees waggle dance create **vibrations**. The fall demands hard work so they must be aware of the dancing communication.

The nuts start to fall and are hid by the squirrels.
The days become short in the northern part of the **world**.

When the days become shorter, the green chlorophyll leaves. Yellow **Xanthophyll** (zan-thuh-fil) becomes visible in autumn trees.

The true color of many leaves are **yellow**, red, and orange that abound. With less sunshine, chlorophyll is hard to be found.

The **zealous** beaver works all night long. The cooling weather pushes him to work until his dam is solid and strong.

Fun Information

Bee Waggle Dance

Bees can fly many miles in a day searching for food. When a bee finds a source of food, it will return to the hive and tell the rest of the bees about its location. It does this by performing a dance. Using the sun as a guide, the bee waggles its body in the direction of the food. The length of the dance tells the rest of the bees how far away the food is. Can you do a dance to tell your parents where the peanut butter is located?

Hibernation

In the winter some animals will make themselves a shelter, known as a den or a burrow. The animal will go inside, its metabolism will slow, and it will "sleep" in order to conserve its body's energy stores. Hibernation makes most people think of bears but do you know that frogs and toads hibernate as well?

Fun Information
Photosynthesis

During the warmer months, leaves produce chlorophyll because there is more sunlight. Chlorophyll soaks up the sunlight like a straw, uses some of the absorbed energy for growth and development of the plant and the rest is stored in other areas like the roots and fruits.. The green color is dominant during the warmer months and hides the other vibrant colors that are waiting to reveal themselves during the fall.

As the days start to shorten and the nights start to lengthen, trees and other plants start to prepare for winter. Trees prepare for winter by stopping flow to and from a leaf's stem in order to save its energy. This is why the green color of leaves fade and the yellow, red and orange colors are displayed during the fall. As the nights continue to get longer trees prepare by losing their leaves. The leaves fall to the ground and provide a protective layer to insulate the roots. The tree can conserve its energy and wait for the warmer days with more sunlight to return.

As the days start to shorten and the nights start to lengthen, trees and other plants start to prepare for winter. Trees prepare for winter by stopping flow to and from a leaf's stem in order to save its energy. This is why the green color of leaves fade and the yellow, red and orange colors are displayed during the fall. As the nights continue to get longer, trees prepare by losing their leaves. The leaves fall to the ground and provide a protective layer to insulate the roots. The tree can conserve its energy and wait for the warmer days with more sunlight to return.

In no way are the sources below affiliated or endorse this book.

Tarragó-Celada, Josep, and Josep M Fernández Novell. "Colour, Chlorophyll and Chromatography." Science in School, 21 June 2019, www.scienceinschool.org/content/colour-chlorophyll-and-chromatography.

National Oceanic and Atmospheric Administration (NOAA). "Cool Autumn Weather Reveals Nature's True Hues." Cool Autumn Weather Reveals Nature's True Hues | National Oceanic and Atmospheric Administration, www.noaa.gov/stories/cool-autumn-weather-reveals-nature-s-true-hues.

Science Made Simple. "Autumn Leaves: How Plants Prepare for Winter by Science Made Simple." Autumn Leaves - How Plants Prepare for Winter, www.sciencemadesimple.com/plants-in-winter.html.

Did you know that certain colors of plants attract bees, other insects and birds for pollination? Honey bees love rosemary, sunflowers, echinacea, lavender, basil and chrysanthemum. You can plant these around your house, even in a pot, to attract these special pollinators. Guess what? You can also eat all of these plants listed in this paragraph. It is important to know that bees, specifically honeybees, pollinate over a third of our food supply and 90% of wild plants. We rely on pollinators to help reproduce many plants. They are so important that some farmers even rent bees to pollinate their crops, if they do not already own bees. Did you know that we are losing bees at an alarming rate? It is called Colony Collapse Disorder (CCD). Let's work together to help take care of our special pollinators. Try your best not to use pesticides or insecticide. Plant organic seeds, make sure that your seeds are not genetically modified (GMO).

About the Authors

We wish that we could give a full embrace to mountains. Since we cannot wrap our arms around them, we climb them to express our love. The harder the mountain demands us to work the more we fall in love with it because, to us, the views at the top are a window into heaven. We feel alive, charged and accomplished.

"Hunger cannot be avoided but the way that you satisfy it can be controlled."
- Christi Salyer

Jason Salyer is an avid outdoorsman/adventurer. He was the Head Strength and Conditioning Coach at the University of California Riverside and a Human Performance Specialist for Naval Special Warfare. Jason's love for teaching gave him the desire to create his YouTube Channel On3 so that he can educate others about the areas that he is most passionate about. His skills and knowledge of the outdoor world was recently tested during an intense challenge on one of History Channel's new shows.

Christi Salyer is an enthusiastic and devoted mother, wife, and Realtor®. She uses her knowledge from her Bachelor's in Business to apply to her personal and professional life. She started writing at a young age. Her mother is a creative storyteller and is one of the influencers on her writing. She uses her energy and humor to encourage others to work hard and to do their best. She demands herself to do the same. She is known to work tirelessly in most areas and rarely is acquainted with the action of quitting. Even when quitting is necessary, like the day that she attempted to twirl as many times as she could while ice skating, slammed onto the ice, giving herself a concussion.

About the Illustrator

Caitlyn Kingsbury is from Cornelius, NC and is actively working in arts education for K-12 students. Beyond illustrating, she enjoys bead weaving, book making, and crocheting. When not drawing or painting, she can be found riding horses, playing with her golden retriever Willow, or enjoying the company of friends over hot tea.

Made in the USA
Columbia, SC
03 December 2020